How To Become Vegan In 7 Days

Dawn Martin, Manhattan Beach, CA

Second Edition

CONTACT

cinderellavegan@mail.com

DISCLAIMER

This book is intended as general information only, and should not be used to diagnose or treat any health condition. This book is not intended to replace professional medical advice. The ideas, procedures and suggestions in this book is the personal opinion of the Author and not provided to replace the advice of a trained medical professional. Consult your physician before adopting any of the suggesions in this book, as well as about any condition that may require diagnosis or medical attention. The Author and publisher disclaim any liability arising directly or indirectly from the use of this book.

DEDICATION

To my Mother Irene Martin

Thank you for trying to satisfy my insatiable appetite for greens and the countless pots of collards and turnips you cleaned and cooked just for me.

ABOUT

Dawn Martin

After suffering debilitating, excruciating, and incapacitating abdominal pain for several years, and not receiving correct diagnosis or help from physicians, Dawn healed herself after becoming Vegan. 2022 marks Dawn's 20th (twentieth) year as a Vegan.

Born and raised in Detroit, Michigan, Dawn is a former Spelling Bee Champion, and was promoted from the 7th to 9th grade. At age 19 Dawn earned an Associate of Arts Degree, and at age 22 she earned a Bachelor's Degree in Journalism then later attended USC Law School but dropped out after one year.

Dawn's was Model of The Year, a Finalist in The Miss Teen USA Pageant and Miss San Francisco.

Dawn has appeared as a Special Guest on Oprah, Geraldo, Phil Donahue, Jenny Jones, Montel, The British TV and more!

Connect

cinderellavegan.com

FAMOUS VEGANS

Prince

Gwyneth Paltrow

Brad Pitt

Erykah Badu

Ed Begley, Jr.

Ellen DeGeneres

Corretta Scott King

Russell Simmons

Pamela Anderson

Steve Wynn

Miley Cyrus

Paul McCartney

Michelle Pfeiffer

LET THY FOOD
BE YOUR MEDICINE

CONTENT
Table of
CHAPTERS

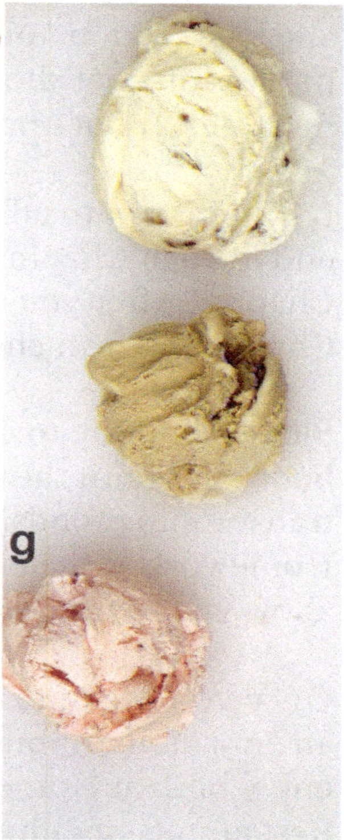

Introduction

This book was written to make the transition from the SAD (Standard American Diet) to becoming 100% Vegan simple and easy. If done properly, you do not need to drag out the process of what should be a simple transition to eating healthier. It does not take 2 weeks or more to become Vegan.

It's important to adhere to the "Homework" outlined at the end of each Chapter BEFORE proceeding to the next Chapter! After you've completed your Homework for each Chapter you can check it off as DONE in the check box.

Please continue to eat your regular foods at the start of this book, and until the Author explains the consumption of transitioning foods, and after you have completed the Homework at the end of each Chapter. Transition foods will allow you to wean off the SAD Diet.

Once you began to explore Vegan foods, you will discover an enormous amount of delicious Vegan foods you can enjoy both at Home and at many of the new Vegan Restaurants opening all over the World!

It seems that more people today are beginning to understand the connection between what you eat and health. I have never before seen so many new Vegan meats, pastries, Restaurants, etc. I do believe that being Vegan is the way the majority of people will eat in the future!

And don't forget to ENJOY the process of your journey from the SAD Diet to eating healthy VEGAN food!

*All photos of food in this book are VEGAN!

DAY 1

EDUCATE YOURSELF

Congratulations on taking the first important step to greatly improving your health by becoming Vegan! As with any lifestyle change, being Vegan requires discipline. There may be times when you become crancky, irritated, anxious, and/or experience withdrawal symptoms. However you must continue to eat healthy to improve your eating habits and health.

The first thing you need to understand is WHY you should become Vegan. Therefore the first you need to do is educate yourself.

Remember: What you eat is more important than anything else you do for your body. Do you actually believe that all the hormones, antibiotics and bacteria from sores on animals disappear once meat companies cover the meat in plastic? Absolutely NOT, because it ends up in your stomach!

Becoming Vegan was easy for me because when I was suffering excruciating, debilitating, incapacitating abdominal attacks after eating the SAD (Standard American Diet). I vowed that if I ever learned what was causing my "attacks", that I'd do anything just to minimize the pain.

To my astonishment, once I became Vegan it was like turning off a switch, because I never again experienced horrible abdominal pain that was worse than labor pains.

I know that forever giving up your favorite foods will be one of the hardest things to do in your life. Growing up in Detroit, Michigan, I enjoyed fast foods like other kids. When my Mother would allow me, I'd enjoy A&W Coney Island Hot Dogs, White Castle Hamburgers, Taco Bell, McDonalds, etc. I used to love beef short ribs, rib eye steaks and other American foods. Now, I would not step on any of the above. Because I educated myself on the truth behind the American Food Industry I don't even crave the things I used to eat. I can watch others eat meat and I do not want it, however to myself I'm thinking how gross it looks. I have learned to never discuss food habits of others, as it will only lead to arguments. Most people *want* to be healthy, but they lack the discipline necessary to attain their goals.

Many people expect things to happen by osmosis, and want to believe that if they purchase a piece of gym equipment, a book or vegetables they will improve their health. These same people end up using their gym equipment for clothes hangers and watch their vegetables rot.

The truth is: You've got to put the work into being Vegan. You've got to do the Homework. You must become Vegan by *your* efforts. Although eating Vegan is semantically referred to as a "diet", even in this book, you've got to understand that being Vegan is NOT a diet, but a way of life!

Many people expect things to happen by osmosis, and want to believe that if they purchase a piece of gym equipment, a book or vegetables will improve their health. These sample people end up using their gym equipment for clothes hangers and watch their vegetables rot.

The truth is: You've got to put the work into being Vegan. You've got to do the Homework. You must become Vegan by *your* efforts. You've got to understand that being Vegan is NOT a diet, as it 's a way of life!

Good News!

Vegans can eat more VOLUME of food and get more nutrients because there are fewer calories in fresh fruit and vegetables than sugared and salted down foods. Many Vegans eat their food either slightly cooked or not cooked at all, because when you cook produce, you lose necessary nutrients and enzymes.

WHAT IS THE DIFFERENCE IN VEGAN, RAW VEGAN & VEGETARIAN?

RAW VEGAN-Is a Vegan who consumes only uncooked produce.

VEGAN- Vegans do not consume animal products or byproducts. Some Vegans do not consume honey or yeast. Many Vegans do not wear clothing made from animal skin.

VEGETARIAN - A person who does not eat meat, and who's diet consists wholly of vegetables, fruits, grains, nuts, and sometimes eggs or dairy products, such as cheese. Vegetarians have less dietary restrictions than Vegans.

ABOUT THE RAW FOOD DIET

- Because of the high fiber, the Raw Food Diet helps prevent cancer and digestive disorders
- Raw Food Diet does not require cooking
- You can create foods that are similar to the SAD (Standard American Diet)

Homework

ASSIGNMENT FOR DAY 1

As soon as possible, watch the movie **Earthlings** in entirety. If you must take a break, STOP the movie and return to it. Do NOT skip over watching any portions! Keep your eyes OPEN and watch it all. Earthlings Movie is only 1 hour and 35 minutes.

Of all the many Vegan movies I've watched, **Earthlings** remain my favorite!

Instead of drinking soda or beer while watching **Earthlings**, try drinking sparkling water with a squeeze of fresh lime or lemon. If you want or need to add sweetener to your beverage, try adding a teaspoon or tablespoon of honey. I have not had soda in over 20 years and do not miss it! I have provided a Youtube link below, however if you're unable to view Earthlings on Youtube, trying renting or purchasing the movie.

Because you need to watch a movie for Day 1 Assignment, we're going to keep this Chapter short.

https://www.youtube.com/watch?v=8gqwpfEcBjI

DAY 2

UNDERSTANDING WHY

Prior to becoming Vegan, I believed Vegans were just elite, snobby, animal activists who were just plain weird and wanted attention. Then I got sick. Very, very sick. For over ten years I suffered death-defying, incapacitating, excruciating painful abdominal attacks that usually occurred 5-20 minutes after eating and left me unresponsive to Paramedics. It was like I was two different people. One minute I was fine, up talking and laughing but within minutes I would be in a fetal position and knowing I was going to die, I would tell whoever was next to me my dying last words.

During my "attacks" my vital signs would sky rocket!

One 911 Report stated:
Blood Pressure was 228/112 with a 120 Pulse. EKG Monitoring and Oxygen administered. Eyes 4 (closed), Motor 6, Verbal 5 (I could no longer talk...just mumble). Whatever I was eating was causing me to die.

I went to top physicians in Beverly Hills, Los Angeles and UCLA. All the doctors I went to misdiagnosed or could not diagnose me.

Because I'm female and was complaining of horrendous pain between my navel and pubic area, two of the doctors ordered that I should have a hysterectomy as soon as possible. One OBGYN told me I just needed a stool softener. It all sounded ridiculous!

One physician wrote in my medical report:
"Patient began to cry when I told her she need an operation ASAP." I literally cried tears because I did not know what to do, and what I was hearing did not make sense and I was not provided any evidence that I needed an operation.

Instead of having an operation I began to immediately research what was causing me to feel like I was dying after I ate the foods I had eaten my entire life. Or was it the food, what was wrong with me?

I initially tried Chinese Herbal teas which tasted so bad I had a mint nearby to plop in my mouth.

After reading several books on how people healed themselves from debilitating medical problems by becoming Vegan, I decided to try Veganism. After all I was desperate to just minimize the intensity of my horrible abdominal pains.

The first day I went grocery shopping, I only shopped in the the produce department and purchased food with ONE ingredient. The first day I only ate Vegan I did not have an attack.

The second day I continued to eat foods with ONE ingredient...a tomato, an apple, Kale, strawberries, and again no attacks, no Paramedics! To make a long story short, instead of my usual 1-3 daily attacks, to my surprise, once I became Vegan I never suffered another attack.

After I became Vegan I felt a true connection to plants, trees and the Earth. When I'd take my morning jog, it was as though the trees and mushrooms were communicating with me. As the trees leaves fluttered in the wind, it felt as though they were telling me, *"We're here if you need us. You're beautiful...We're beautiful. You can relax near us. We're here to heal you and keep you strong. If others took the time, they'd know the answer too."*

I believe the SAD manifest differently in people. Some people contract diabetes, gout, heart disease, cancer and other illnesses. In my case, I experienced horrendous abdominal pains worse than labor pains. And unlike labor pains wherein you have contractions, my pain was constant. In retrospect, I feel the horrible abdominal pains I suffered was a blessing in disguise, because after educating myself, I would not eat the SAD even if I could!

Before you initiate anything, you must understand and ask yourself WHY you are doing so. Once I started studying the link between diet and illness, I quickly learned that the food industry, primarily the meat and dairy industry is corrupt.

Cows, pigs and chickens are pumped full of steroids, growth hormones, antibiotics and more, all of which stays in the animals. Therefore when you eat beef, pork, chicken, lamb or any animal flesh you're also consuming enough of the steroids, growth hormones antibiotics, etc., to cause an array of health problems. I believed this is what caused my abdominal "attacks".

Cows, chickens, turkeys and pigs throats are slit when they're fully conscious. Dairy cows are so sick and weak they're unable to walk or stand, yet they're slaughtered for milk.

The method of producing meat is disgusting!

Going Vegan to lose weight is far better than gastric bypass or lap band surgery because in both, there is a vitamin deficiency, since fewer nutrients are absorbed, resulting in patients requiring supplements and possibly prescription drugs.

What Physicians Don't Know & Won't Tell You!

Did you know that the majority of Physicians only receive approximately one hour of education in nutrition in medical school? Medical students do not spend hundreds of thousands of dollars to study about vitamins and alternative healing or healing with food.

Medical students study how to heal with drugs and surgery! Once I learned this, I realized why all the physicians I went to regarding my excruciating, incapacitating and debilitating abdominal pain recommended immediate surgery to remove any and all of my female organs, and prescribed me Vicodin to take for pain. I hate drugs, but because my abdominal pain was causing me to have difficulty breathing, moving, and walking and talking, I would bite the Vicodin in half, then soon fall asleep. I was amazed when I awoke because it was hard to believe I was still alive after enduring such horrendous pain.

Even if I had spent approximately $120,000 for the hysterectomy all the physicians told me I needed, I'd still have the horrible abdominal pain in addition to a bad surgical scar, because surgery would NOT have solved my problem. Luckily, to this day I've NEVER had any surgeries!

So in addition to being educated to push drugs, most physicians do not know how to heal the human body naturally, so they can't tell you because they simply don't know, and many do not want to learn how to heal naturally.

And the few physicians that do know about nutrition because they've learned on their own, will be ostracized by their peers and governing agencies for not abiding by "medical guidelines".

Do you realize that physicians can "guarantee" very little or nothing? Doctors are just "practicing" medicine.

Many pharmaceutical companies sponsor and donate to various medical industries and professionals.

Pharmaceutical companies bombard physician and dental offices with prescription "samples". Haven't you ever had your physician or dentist gift you with prescription samples like dermatological creams, pain killers, and other samples like aspirins, toothpaste, etc.? It's because medical professionals receive samples from pharmaceutical and dental companies all the time!

WHY SHOULD YOU CARE?

Many animals are born indoors and never leave the building they're raised in until they're slaughtered. Most animals and chickens are so confined that they can barely move, causing festering sores that are difficult or impossible to heal. Why would you want to EAT an animal that had open sores and disease?!

Cows are fed genetically modified corn and soy which they would never eat in the wild. Cows have a digestive system for digesting grass, yet they are pumped full of drugs to help digest food their digestive system would not otherwise handle.

Farmed fish are raised in filthy pools and fed corn because it's a cheap method of feedings. Fish would never eat CORN if their farmers did not fed it to them!

Oceans are polluted with urine, feces, dead bodies, ships, planes, fuel, dead animals, etc., so any fish you eat is most likely contaminated. Tuna has heavy metals and when you eat tuna, the metals do not disappear. In the middle of the Pacific Ocean is a huge sludge of trash larger than the State of Texas produced by humans. The oceanic trash dump contains plastic bottles, furniture, TV's etc. No county has ever taken responsibility for the oceanic dump and every year it gets bigger. Poisons from the oceanic trash contaminate seafood.

The Pharmacy

- Animal products and byproducts are unnecessary.
- What you eat is a learned habit, so eat HEALTHY!
- You will be healthier if you do not eat meat and dairy.
- Animal products and byproducts are unnecessary.
- Eating Vegan is environmentally friendly.
- More people can be fed on a plant diet than animal.
- For religion and/or spiritual reasons. "Thou shall kill."
- Saves money! Produce is cheaper than meat!
- Vegan food taste great!
-

Why Dawn Became Vegan

- I wanted to reduce the intensity of my horrible abdominal pain!
- I wanted my life back because my attacks were affecting every aspect of my life and time.

On the following page, list why YOU want to be Vegan!
At this time, you can continue to eat as usual if desired.

Homework

ASSIGNMENT FOR DAY 2

- On the next page list your interest and reasons for wanting to become Vegan.

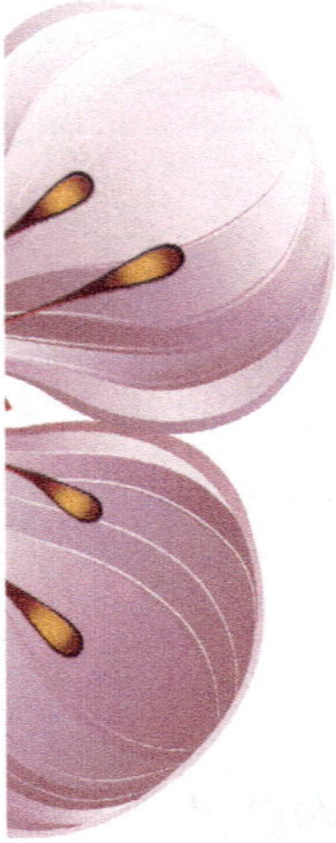

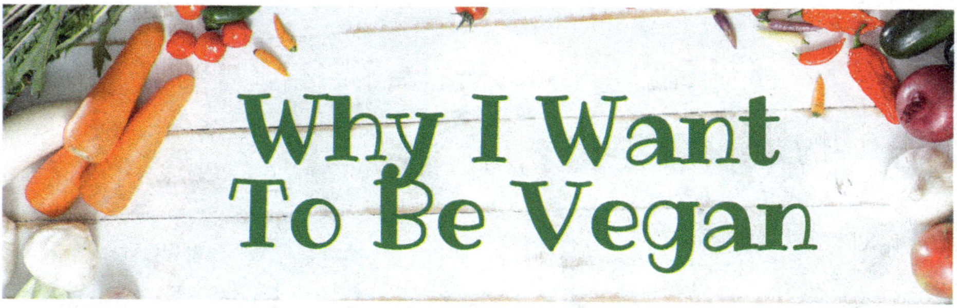

Why I Want To Be Vegan

3

WEANING OFF/DETOXING WHAT AMERICANS CAN LEARN FROM THE JAPANESE

1 out of every 3 people are overweight in the United States. Men look pregnant. When I was in Japan I saw one overweight Japanese person, which was a woman at the Narita Airport. Maybe she was visiting from the United States?

Hara hachi bu is a cultural habit practiced ont he Island of Okinawa, Japan. Okinawans live longer and are healthier than any other people on Earth. One reason for their longevity is that they eat fewer calories than the average person. This calorie restriction combined with plenty of fruits and vegetables resuts in less damage by free radicals.

Hari hachi bu is an easy to follow principle in Japan because food portions are much smaller than in places like the United States. Using chopsticks also makes it easier to avoid shoveling food in your mouth because it encourages eating at a slower pace.

Hara hachi bu does not encourage wastefulness and it does not mean leave 20% of your meal on your plate.

If you stop eating before getting 100% full, you will be more satisfied with your meal, not sleepy afterwards and generally feel better after eating, than when you overeat.

In Okinawa, heart disease and strokes rates are 80% lower than in the United States. Blood pressure, cholesterol and homocystein levels are lower in Japan than in the United States.

Rates of Cancer are 50% - 80% lower in Japan, especially breast, colon, ovarian and prostate cancer. Dementia is rare in Japan and hip fractures are 20% lower in Japan than in the United States.

Regular, life-long physical activiites such as Tai Chi, walking and gardening are common forms of exercise in Japan.

Reward yourself when you have maintained your new healthy way of eating. But even when rewarding yourself, you should stay Vegan and pracice Hara hachi bu! There are many delicious Vegan pastries like chocolate chip cookes and Vegan chocolate bars and Vegan ice cream...just don't overeat!

SEVEN SECRETS OF THE JAPANESE KITCHEN

- Portions are small
- Cooking is light
- Desserts are teeny-tiny
- Japanese women don't go on "diets", but rather eat small amounts of whatever they like.
- Rice replaces bread
- Breakfast is powered by Miso Soup
- Preferred foods include fish, vegetables, fruit, soy & rice

HOW JAPANESE EATING WORKS

Japanese is about cooking simple meals based on fish, vegetables and fruit. The Japanese style is that each food is served in it's own dish and when it comes to portions, less is more! The idea is not to stuff yourself, but to eat until you're 80% full or less than 80% full.

Food presentation is very important when you're Vegan. Because you're sacrificing favorite foods from the SAD (Standard American Diet), you've got to make your Vegan presentation exceptional!

REMEMBER

- Never fill-up your plate
- Forgo super-size portions!
- Less is more
- Fresh is best!

THE BEAUTIFUL JAPANESE BENTO BOX

The aesthetics of food is very important in Japan and Bento is the aesthetic presentation of food in a box, while calling for food to remain in their natural state. Food should be made into recognizable shapes that evoke nature, like animal or flower shapes. Bento Boxes can be decorated with natural objects such as real flowers or leaves. In Japan Mothers often prepare their children's Bento Box every morning with creativity. Portions are small and usually one tenth the size of American average portions. Sadly, in the United States many people eat "super size" portions.

The Bento Box can be a valuable tool when you're Vegan. Firstly, you will find that you're usually packing snacks or meals on the go. And after a little practice you will soon be able to easily prepare a very beautiful and delicious Bento Box!

BENTO BOX of
Crispy Tofu with Rice & Salad

You can purchase Bento Boxes or use containers you already have in your kitchen like Tupperware.

DO'S

1. Drink beverages out of glass, not plastic because exposure to plastics increases estrogen levels.
2. Eat organic fruits and vegetables.
3. Start out becoming Vegan *SLOWLY* or you will become frustrated and quit.
4. CLEANSE. Juicing is a great way to initiate a detox and internal cleansing regime. Another great way to start detoxing is by eating ORGANIC produce for several days. You can basically eat as much as you like of apples, grapes, watermelon, spinach, kale, etc.
5. Get sufficient sleep.
6. Get enough exercise.
7. Use Himalayan Salt. Never use table salt.
8. Drink enough pure water.
9. Eat plenty of FRESH vegetables and fruit.
10. Instead of using soy sauce, use Coconut Amino Acids which taste very similar to soy sauce but it's healthy for you.

DON'T

1. Don't eat bad, junk food and animals foods and byproducts.
2. Don't eat Vegan recipes that are really 100% fat like cheesecake mainly made from nuts.
3. Don't smother natural flavors with condiments or oils.
4. Don't eat too many concentrated sweets like honey or maple syrup.
5. Don't worry or frequently think about food.
6. Don't consume too much oil. (This includes olive, flax seed, coconut oils, etc.)
7. Don't eat processed foods.
8. Don't eat packaged dairy products.
9. Don't eat white flour products.
10. Don't eat genetically modified foods.

PRODUCE STICKERS

It's very important that you read and pay attention to the little stickers on produce. If the produce sticker has a code that begins with a 4, it was grown conventionally. If it begins with a 9, it was grown organically. If it begins with an 8, it's GMO. GMOs are foods modified and grown with chemicals. Do NOT eat GMOs.

Homework

<u>ASSIGNMENT FOR DAY 3</u>

- Announce to friends and family that you're improving your health and no longer eat meat or meat byproducts such as dairy.
- Inform your friends and family to please under no circumstances offer or purchase you any meat or meat byproducts.
- CLEAN OUT YOUR REFRIGERATOR AND KITCHEN CABINETS.
- Eat what you want from your kitchen, even SAD food, and donate or trash what you no longer want, however after watching Earthlings Movie you probably will not want to eat from the SAD diet.
- If you live with others make a special shelf in the refrigerator and cabinets for your Vegan foods.

4

TRANSITION FOODS

When other people tell me they could never be Vegan, I immediately know it's because "they don't know how to maintain being Vegan!" If only they started off correctly! We're here to DO IT RIGHT! If I can remain Vegan for 20 (twenty) years so can you! As a matter of fact I wish I'd been Vegan my entire life!

WHAT ABOUT PROTEIN?

Have you ever heard of anyone becoming ill from a protein deficiency? It's a myth that we need massive amounts of protein. Too much protein, especially animal protein can impair kidneys, leach calcium, zinc, vitamin B, iron and magnesium from our bodies, and also cause osteoporosis, heart disease, cancer and obesity. High amounts of protein can damage tissues, organs and cells and contribute to aging.

Some Americans are obsessed with protein. Vegans are bombarded with questions about where we get our protein. this concern about protein is misplaced. Protein is certainly an essential nutrient which plays many key roles in the way our bodies function but we don't need huge quantities.

Horses, cows, deer, elephants and gorillas are naturally vegetarians. Where does all their muscle and body mass come from? Grass and leafy greens, and for gorillas, it's fruit!

If you eat plant based whole foods each day you will not lack in protein.

<u>How To Figure Your Protein Needs</u>

An average size person (no out-of-the-ordinary physique) needs approximately 1 gram of protein per kilogram of body weight. One pound equals .45 kilograms. To figure how many kilograms you weigh simply multiply your weight by .45. So if you weight 105 pounds that means you weigh .47.6 kilograms. Since an average person needs approximately 1 gram of protein per kilogram of body weight, then you would aim for around 47 grams of protein per day.

If you eat lentils, beans, nuts, seeds, fruits, vegetables, whole grains and well-balanced meals, you are guaranteed to get sufficient protein. However, fruit does not have much protein.

In his book Optimal Health, Dr. Patrick Holford explains: *"Most people are in more danger of eating too much protein than too little."* Educated Vegans always laugh when questioned about where we get our protein.

Vegan athletes may have higher protein needs than Vegans who exercise moderately or who are not active.

GOOD VEGAN PROTEIN FOODS

BEANS

BROWN RICE

OATMEAL

PEANUT BUTTER

KALE

SPROUTS

BROCCOLI

HEMP SEEDS

FLAX SEEDS

PUMPKIN SEEDS

ALMONDS

SPINACH

QUINOA

LENTILS

PEAS

Vegan Protein
SOURCES CHART

GF Gluten-Free
SF Soy-Free
NF Nut Free

BEANS
1/2 CUP
GF SF NF

- Lentils 7g
- Chickpeas 7g
- Black Beans 7g

SOY
1/2 CUP
GF NF

- Tempeh 15g
- Tofu 10g
- Edamame (Shelled) 9g
- Soy Milk 7g

NUTS
2 TBSP
GF SF

- Nut Butters 7g
- Walnuts 4g
- Peanuts 3.5g
- Almonds 3g
- Pistachios (Shelled) 3g

SEEDS
2 TBSP
GF SF NF

- Pepitas 8g
- SunButter 7g
- Hemp Hearts 7g
- Sunflower Seeds (Shelled) 5g
- Chia Seeds 5g

GRAINS
1/2 CUP
SF NF

- Whole wheat spaghetti 12g
- Rolled oats 7g
- Ezekiel bread 4g

GLUTEN FREE
1/2 CUP
GF SF

- GF chickpea pasta 22g
- GF lentil pasta 15g
- GF rolled oats 7g
- Quinoa 4g

VEGGIES
1 CUP
GF SF NF

- Green Peas 8g
- Spinach (cooked) 5g
- Potato with skin (large) 4g
- Broccoli 3g

Always check labels for allergen information!.
Nutritional data and servings obtained from USDA Nutrient Database and product packaging.

IRON

Iron is an essential mineral because it contributes to the production of blood cells. The human body needs iron to make the oxygen-carrying proteins hemoglobin and myoglobin. But just because you don't eat meat doesn't mean you're going to wither away with anemia.

According to the World Heath Organization (WHO), 80% of the World's population may be iron deficient, while 30% may have iron deficiency anemia. Low iron levels over a long period of time can lead to iron deficiency anemia.

HIGHEST IRON PLANT BASED FOODS

Spirulina (1tsp)	5 mg
Pumpkin Seeds (1 ounce)	4.2 mg
Quinoa (4 ounces)	4 mg
Blackstrap Molasses (1 tbsp)	4 mg
White beans (1/2 cup)	3.9 mg
Cooked spinach (1/2 cup)	3.2 mg
Dried peaches	3.1 mg
Prune juice	3 mg
Lentils	3 mg

IRON REQUIREMENTS

The Food & Nutrition Board at the Institute of Medicine recommends the following:

Daily Iron Milligram Requirement

	Male	Female	Pregnancy	Lactation
Birth to 6 months	0.27 mg*	0.27 mg*		
7–12 months	11 mg	11 mg		
1–3 years	7 mg	7 mg		
4–8 years	10 mg	10 mg		
9–13 years	8 mg	8 mg		
14–18 years	11 mg	15 mg	27 mg	10 mg
19–50 years	8 mg	18 mg	27 mg	9 mg
51+ years	8 mg	8 mg		

TIPS TO GET THE MOST IRON OUT OF YOUR FOOD

- Eat iron rich foods along with foods that contain vitamin C, which helps the body absorb iron.

- Tea and coffee contains compounds called polyphenols which can bind with iron, making it harder for our bodies to absorb iron. Calcium also hinders the absorption of iron, so avoid high calcium foods for half an hour before or after eating iron rich foods.

- Anemia results mainly because of iron deficiency. Anemia is caused by being deficient in folic acid and Vitamin B 12.

- A Vitamin B12 deficiency can lead to anemia, constipation, weakness, loss of appetite, weight loss, depression confusion, dementia, poor memory, soreness of the mouth or tongue and irreversible nerve damage such as tingling and numbness in the hands and feet.

RELIABLE WAYS TO GET VITAMIN B12

Vegan B12 Supplements - Your supplement should be "sublingual", meaning it melts under the tongue.

Just one table of Nutritional Yeast provides 40% of the Daily Value for Vitamin B 12. In addition to being a good source of Vitamin B 12 is rich in B complex vitamins Thiamin (B 1), Riboflavin (B 2), Niacin (B3), Pyridoxine (B 6), Folic Acid and Pantothenic Acid. Nutritional yeast is also a source for zinc and selenium.

Nutritional Yeast

WHAT ABOUT FATS?

Flax seed oil, alive oil, almonds, walnuts, almond butter and avocados all contain healthy fats. For optimal health some saturated fat is required, so get some coconut oil or coconut milk in your diet as well.

If you're body building, make sure you eat a variety of foods while transitioning from the SAD to Vegan way of eating, so you can get a full array of muscle building amino acids. Some good choices are black beans quinoa, lentils brown rice, almond butter, rice protein, soy milk, green peas, etc. Have veggie burgers or other faux meat products occasionally, but make sure you mainly eat fresh organic produce.

TASTY VEGAN MOCK MEATS

There are more Vegan Restaurants and companies producing Vegan meat than ever before!

When I became Vegan 20 years ago I had fewer options!

When transitioning from the SAD Diet to becoming Vegan, "Transition Foods" is the way to go!

I went Vegan immediately because I needed to escape my horrible abdominal attacks that left me unresponsive to Paramedics with difficulty breathing, and the inability to talk or walk. I cannot cheat and eat SAD foods.

TRANSITIONING TO VEGAN

Although my Vegan lifestyle of eating consists 80% of fresh organic produce made from scratch, I sometimes have a craving for Vegan prepared foods.

I HAVE LISTED SOME OF MY VEGAN PREPARED & FROZEN FOODS BELOW! YES, yes, yes, I have personally tried ALL of the below foods, and although I'm a "picky" eater I must say that ALL the foods on the next few pages are delicious! I am NOT getting paid to list any of the transition foods, but simply wanted to share my "favorites".

Not only must my food be 100% Vegan, but it has to also be delicious! In my 20 (twenty) year experience as a Vegan, rather than rely on Vegan Recipe books, I prefer to come up with my own Vegan Recipes.

So with this in mind, I am not telling you to rush and purchase a new Vegan Recipe book, because if you don't like the recipe or something goes wrong in the preparation, it may discourage you from attaining your goal.

I have created Homework for this Chapter, so that you can explore what's available for quick and convenient Vegan meals for yourself or the whole family.

Even as a 20 year Vegan I sometimes enjoy eating my favorite quick and easy Vegan meals I've listed in this Chapter. Although considered "transition Vegan Meals", you can still enjoy them long after being Vegan.

Quick delicious breakfast!
Can take to work & heat.

Delicious in beans or on bread as a sandwich. Can also put on toothpicks with pineapple & serve as an appetizer.

Love these!

Delicious with Kale
or your favorite beans.

Delicious!...Can't tell the difference from SAD eggs.

Taste BETTER than real meat! Needs NO seasoning. Delicious with Just Eggs

Actual photo of
Soft Serve Ice Cream Cone
I shot in my car! Orange Dole
Whip & Vanilla Swirl.
It TASTE much, much, much
better than it looks!

SO Delicious VEGAN Ice Cream
made from Cashews!

Homework

ASSIGNMENT FOR DAY 4

- Enjoy a quick and tasty Vegan Dinner tonight. Visit your local major chain grocery store such as: Whole Foods, Sprouts, Albertsons or Smiths. All the major chain grocery stores usually carry 100% Vegan frozen meals. Target and Walmart also now carry many name brand Vegan meals.

Before selecting your Vegan meal, you should browse the entire Vegan frozen food section to see what you prefer.

The above grocery stores may also have 100% Vegan frozen pizza.

Whole Foods has fresh Vegan pizza that's delicious. You can also order fresh 100% Vegan sandwiches from Whole Foods.
I thoroughly enjoy the TLT Sandwhich at Whole Foods!...It's so delicious that it was recently a Youtube sensation! You should try it! You can select whatever fresh bread you want too. The TLT or mock BLT is made with tempeh.

5

DINING OUT & SOCIALIZNG

It's important that I enjoy everything I eat. Prior to becoming Vegan, except for my Mother's greens, I considered vegetables boring and tasteless, and did not eat many vegetables. Now I LOVE Vegetables and love being Vegan!

I want to enjoy every morsel I eat, so I've also learned to modify Vegan recipes to my liking. When I first became Vegan I discovered a way to make my green juices bursting with flavor. My secret is that I add my favorite frozen fruit, which quickly turns a boring green drink into a delicious smoothie. If your green drink is not sweet enough, trying adding apple juice or a little honey. I haven't used honey in a while because I've discovered monk fruit sweetener which has no-calories and no effect on blood sugar levels. NEVER USE SUGAR!

THE KEY IN MAINTAINING YOUR VEGAN LIFESTYLE ARE 2 THINGS

1. **Knowing what vegetables and fruits are your favorite &**
2. **Not allowing others to influence what you eat!**

It's necessary to initially tell your family and friends you're Vegan, however some people will seem more interested in your eating lifestyle than their own. Many will act like they are what I call "The Vegan Police". They will question you on what you're eating, yet these same people eat what I would not step on!

Telling someone you're Vegan once is enough. If anyone continues to question you about what you eat, I would simply say "I've already discussed that or I've already told you I'm Vegan. Please do not force your eating habits on me, and I won't force my eating habits on you." If the person or people continue I just ignore them, because it's clear they are attempting to take the conversation in a direction I do not want.

SAVE YOUR ENERGY don't argue about your Vegan Lifestyle. I rarely tell people I'm Vegan. If the conversation comes up and I want to share information I will, but I will not get into an argument over what is my business.

I have learned that some people want to test your willpower and will offer and buy you food that you stated you no longer eat. You must remain strong and stern and tell the person offering you food to get you off your track, to stop offering and/or buying you food.

REAL LIFE VEGAN SCENARIOS

- **Personal Note** - Whether you're just going shopping, on a date, traveling, going to a Party, etc., what I've learned as a Vegan is "It's always best to eat a little something before you leave" because there's no guarantee you will want anyone's Vegan options".

- **Dating** - When accepting a first date with a guy or woman, and your date invites you to dinner, the best thing is not to mention you're Vegan. If you start out giving the impression that everything related to food must be Vegan he/she may get the impression that you're difficult and a long-term relationship is impossible (provided he/she is not Vegan). If you accept the date, allow the guy to select the Restaurant. If he/she insist that you select the Restaurant then you can ask him/her if it's okay if you select a Vegan Restaurant. If you feel your date is "worth it to pursue", and he/she does not want to go to a Vegan restaurant, you can simply go to the restaurant of their choosing and order something from the Menu that is Vegan, such as salad or pasta with vegetables or roasted vegetables. I personally would not date a man that is too selfish to at least try my way of eating.

- **At The Airport** - When I travel, because of TSA restrictions I no longer carry or pack food. TSA used to stop me because when my luggage was scanned my Vegan food would show up in xrays and I would get stopped, and TSA would rummage through my luggage. So now when I travel I either find some type of snack at the Airport shops or simply consider myself not eating during traveling as "intermittent fasting" which is actually good. So, I give my digestion a break until I arrive at my destination where I know I can eat Vegan food of my choosing!

REAL LIFE VEGAN SCENARIOS CONTINUED

- **Wedding Parties** - Contact the Host at least one month before her Event and tell her you're Vegan, and ask if she can accommodate you by having Vegan options available. You might want to mention that Veganism is more popular today than ever, and others in attendance may want to also have Vegan options. If you really want to attend the wedding party and the Host refuses to have Vegan options available, do tell her before hand that you will bring your own Vegan meal. Make sure you have a beautifully prepared meal, perhaps in a beautiful Bento Box. I can assure you if you make your Vegan meal aesthetically beautiful people will be gazing over at you, and asking you all about your meal, where it came from, what is it, etc. Did I tell you I do NOT share my Vegan food particularly when out! Basically because I cannot cheat or run into a fast food place, because if I cannot eat Vegan I don't eat. My food is literally my medicine and I cannot share my medicine! Another reason I don't share is because my Vegan food is too hard to come by, as I have to shop specifically for Vegan food instead of any local market and grab whatever is convenient.

- **Picnics** - Basically the same attitude as Dating.

- **Family Holiday Gatherings** - Basically the same attitude as in Wedding Parties applies here.

- **Grabbing Lunch with Friends** - Basically the same attitude as stated in Dating applies here.

- **Long Car Trips** - Car trips are usually casual so feel free to bring your own meals. If it's a bus ride with friends or family, you can ask the Host if Vegan options will be available. Personally, unless I want to dine at one of my favorite Vegan restaurants, I like preparing my own Vegan meals regardless of the situation.

WE ARE GOING TO DO THIS SAD TO VEGAN TRANSITION RIGHT!

So, let me tell you about the equipment you will definitely require to be a success!

Fortunately, you will be able to purchase all the adequate kitchen necessities for less than $150. If you decide you want upgraded or more expensive products for your Vegan kitchen, of course they will cost more than $150. When I first became Vegan I thought I needed the best of everything and purchased a $700 juicer, a $400 blender, a dehydrator, food processors, etc. Come to find out, I did not like dried out fruit or vegetables and sold my expensive dehydrator. I also sold my $700 juicer and now use a juicer that cost $80, and it's more practical because it's small, much easier to clean and I can literally take it with me when I travel. After two years, I have not had to repair or replace it, and I juice carrots, apples, etc., on a regular basis with my $80 juicer. If I did have to replace my juicer I'd happily do so because it was only $80 and I've used it a lot. I honestly enjoy using and love my less expensive juicer more than the $700 I had because it took too long to clean and was heavy.

Also, my cheaper juicer has is a Cold Press Slow Masticating Juicer Extractor that's very easy to clean, and it came with a frozen attachment to make soft serve ice cream, a cleaning brush, a pulp dispensing, a juice collecting cup and Recipe Guide. Lucky you, as I have shared the link to where you can purchase my amazing $80 juicer at the Resource Guide at the end of this book...and oh, it's available in two colors!

EQUIPMENT YOU NEED TO SUCCEED AS A VEGAN

1. **Juicer** - A good, reliable juicer. I usually purchase juice from the Juice Bar at Whole Foods or ready made 100% Organic orange juice and beet juice at Whole Foods. Beets produce very dry pulp when juicing, so I like to have Whole Foods juice my beets or purchase ready made beet juice. I regularly enjoy juicing carrots at Home.

2. **Blender** - A good, reliable blender. Okay, my blender is soooo reliable, as it should be because I paid $325 for it, but I've have had it for 20 years and have never had a problem with it. If I was just starting out and needed a blender, I'd definitely purchase the same brand!

3. **Food Processor** - I purchased mine for $30 and love it.

4. **A Good Sharp Knife**

5. **A Cutting Board** - You can get one at a Dollar Store

6. **Bento Box** - Both men and women need a great Bento Box. I have several and even have a Stainless Steel Bento Box, if I need to heat food directly in my Bento Box.

7. **Lunch Bag** - One or two nice lunch bags for when you don't want to carry your Bento Box and just want to throw some items and beverages in a bag!

Homework

<u>ASSIGNMENT FOR DAY 5</u>

- Go to happycow.net and find a Vegan Restaurant in your area. Whether traveling internationally or locally, happycow.net is a truly fantastic site to discover a Vegan Restaurant near you. On happycow.net, you can check out their Reviews and see photos of all the delicious Vegan food you can eat BEFORE you order. Bon Appetit!

- You want to know what I enjoy, I like hanging around other long-time Vegans! Before or after you enjoy your dining out, you can find a Vegan Group to join. You can share ideas, learn to prepare new Vegan recipes and make new friends that enjoy your lifestyle of eating. You can start by checking out meetup.com or Facebook and search for Vegans in your area. There's plenty of Vegan Groups on the Internet that meet to discuss new trends in Veganism, new Restaurants, etc.

- If you don't like the Vegan meetups on meetup.com, you can easily <u>start your own Vegan Group</u> and meet up in person or via Zoom. You will feel the comfort of being amongst others that share your way of healthy eating. As with anything in life, be cautious and be safe! If you're going somewhere for the first time, take a friend or relative with you, even if that person is not Vegan because they are with you for protection not to eat Vegan food unless they want.

6

GROCERY SHOPPING & PLANNING YOUR MEALS

It's important that I enjoy everything I eat. Prior to becoming Vegan, except for my Mother's greens, I considered vegetables boring and tasteless, and did not eat many vegetables. Now I LOVE Vegetables and love being Vegan!

I'm so glad I learned how to select and prepare numerous delicious Vegan dishes. After trying other Vegan recipes and eating at Vegan restaurants I enjoy my recipes more.

I want to enjoy every morsel I eat, so I've also learned to modify Vegan recipes to my liking. When I first became Vegan I discovered a way to make my green juices bursting with flavor. My secret is that I add my favorite frozen fruit, which quickly turns a boring green drink into a delicious smoothie. If your green drink is not sweet enough, trying adding apple juice or a little honey. I haven't used honey in a while because I've discovered monk fruit sweetener which has no-calories and no effect on blood sugar levels. NEVER USE SUGAR!

ARTIFICIAL SWEETENERS

Most people use artificial sweeteners to either lose weight or because they are diabetic and must avoid sugar. The main problem is that numerous studies show that people who consume artificial sweeteners on a regular basis, such as in sodas or coffee actually gain weight. Eating artificial sweeteners does little or nothing to help people with diabetes.

In fact artificial sweeteners makes it more difficult to control blood sugar levels and worsen conditions that are related to diabetes such as cataracts. Aspartame has been found to cause convulsions which some people mistake for an insulin reaction.

Chemicals that make up artificial sweeteners, especially aspartame, break down in the body into a deadly toxin called DKP. When your stomach process DKP, it produces chemicals that can cause cancer, especially brain tumors.

Artificial sweeteners inhibit your body's ability to monitor its daily calorie consumption and makes the body crave more sweets!

CANNED TOMATOES

Endocrinologist Fredrick vom Saal, PhD at the University of Missouri, studies bisphenol-A and says:

"The resin linings of tin cans contain bisphenol-A, a synthetic estrogen that has been linked to ailments ranging from reproductive problems, to heart disease, diabetes and obesity. Acidity of tomatoes causes BPA to leach into your food. You can get 50 mcg of BPA per litter out of a tomato can, and that level impacts people, particularly the young. I won't go near canned tomatoes."

DO'S

- Learn how to properly store vegetables & fruits
- Know what your favorite fruits and vegetables are
- Do not eat vegetables or fruit you do not like, as doing so will steer you off a Vegan path.
- Make sure your favorite fruits and vegetables are a staple in your Home & on Grocery List

SOME OF DAWN'S VEGAN SECRETS!

- Grind sun-dried tomatoes and put in soups or salad dressing for a burst of flavor!
- Avocado makes smoothies creamier! Using avocado in foods is similar to tofu because avocados take on any flavor you want. I've made chocolate pudding out of avocados and the SAD eater can't tell the difference!
- Do not soak produce or nuts too long because it reduces the flavor.

FOOD PREPARATION TIPS

- Remove the twist-tie from your produce. This prevents bruising and damage to your produce.

- As soon as you get Home, remove any plastic containers, bags and plastic from your produce! Keeping your produce in plastic causes it to sweat and mold quicker, which decreases the lifespan, and once your produce molds you need to quickly throw it away to make sure there is no contact with other produce.

- Do NOT break apart your lettuce or other produce from the core, vine, etc., until you're ready to use it, because doing so separates the produce from it's life force!

- Because I purchase a large quantity of produce, I simply lay out an organic cotton flour towel at the bottom of my vegetable bin. Then I lay all my produce on top and cover with another organic cotton flour towel. I love flour towels because their thin so produce can breath, and their 100% natural cotton. I also cut the stems of Kale or other similar produce such as lettuce and put it in a jar of water until time to use.

PLAN YOUR MEALS

You certainly do not have to purchase everything on the below grocery list, but it's just to show you many items that Vegans choose from when grocery shopping. Notice that the below list does not contain beets because I'm not a fan of them. Although I am starting to enjoy beet juice with lemon juice because I've discovered that lemon juice drowns out the flavor of beets. I want to drink beet juice because beets are very good for you. Start with a few items and build as you go. Do not try to load up on a lot of vegetables and fruits. I usually shop every 2 - 3 days because I want my produce fresh. I no longer like shopping for clothes or furniture since I've become Vegan, however I actually enjoy grocery shopping!

SOME OF DAWN'S FAVORITES!

I love Sprouts! No matter where you live, try to grow at least one vegetable on your windowsill or patio, even if it's mint. Growing something you eat will give you appreciation for it. You can grow sprouts in a jar and you don't even need dirt!

I love fresh homemade hummus! Fresh vegetables such as celery, or cucumbers can serve as excellent scoops! You can also enjoy hummus with your favorite cracker. Many Vegans enjoy hummus with pita bread.

I've always loved Oranges. Either just cut in quarters as a snack or made into fresh orange juice! It's like liquid sunshine! Slowly sipping fresh squeezed juice is best...never gulp, or you'll miss the excitement!

I LOVE pineapple! Great in a smoothie, grilled, a salad, and array of dishes! Pineapple contains the enzyme, bromelain, which has medicinal properties.

FLU SHOT

Did you know you can make delicious & healthy ice cream from avocados?

Delicious and beautiful Acai bowl

THE NATURAL PHARMACY IS AMAZING!

*A sliced carrot looks like a Human eye and it generally enhances blood flow to the eye.

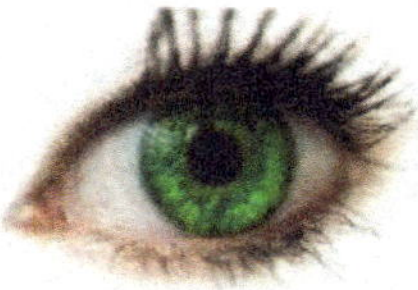

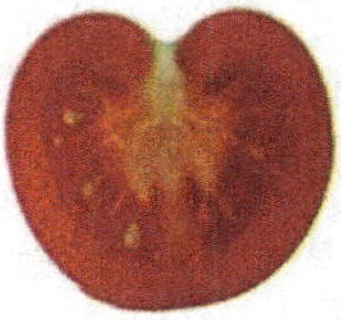

*A tomato has 4 chambers & is red just like the heart . A tomato is loaded with Lycopine that is pure heart & blood food.

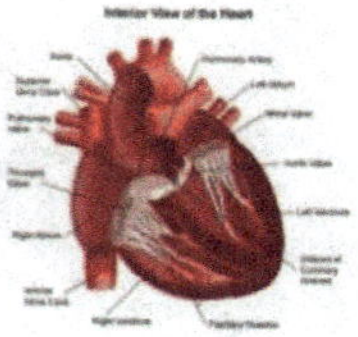

*A walnut looks like a the brain and helps develop more than 3 dozen neuro brain functions.

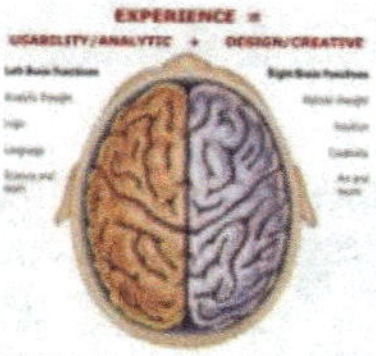

*Beans are kidney shaped and they heal and helps maintain kidney function.

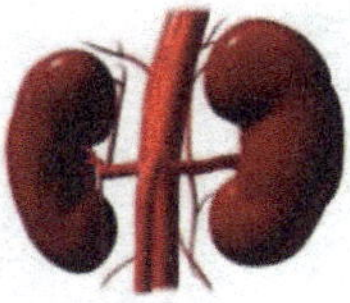

Delicious!

You are going to have so much FUN making make delicious & healthy Beverages for yourself and possibly your family & friends! When I became Vegan it was like I discovered a different world. I enjoyed making new healthy & delicious new meals!

Vegan Beverages are not only delicious but NATURALLY beautiful!

DAWN'S VEGAN MEAL PLAN

ALL IS FOOD IS 100% VEGAN

OCTOBER

MONDAY - FRIDAY

FREE DAYS ON SATURDAY - SUNDAY

	BREAKFAST	LUNCH	DINNER
MON	OATMEAL W/ BANANAS AGAVE GRANOLA	ROASTED SWEET POTATO KALE SALAD	STIR-FRIED VEGETABLES & SESAME NOODLES
TUE	SMOOTHIE W/ FRESH PINEAPPLE & NUT MILK	STIR-FRIED VEGETABLES & MUSHROOMS	ROASTED SWEET POTATO & KALE SALAD JUICE
WED	CORN PUFFS W/ NUT MILK & FRESH FRUIT	STEAMED KALE W/ HUMMUS	SPAGHETTI & MEATBALLS W/ SMALL SALAD
THU	OMELETTE W/ SAUSAGE, SPINACH, TOMATOES & SCRAMBLED TOFU	STEAMED BROCCOLI W/TOMATOES & HUMMUS	VEGAN HAMBURGER & SMALL SALAD W/ DRESSING
FRI	SAUSAGE, TOFU, CHEESE & TOMATO BURRITO	CHICKEN SANDWHICH W/ ROASTED VEGETABLES	VEGAN MACARONI & CHEESE W/ SMALL SALAD

SNACKS: Fresh Fruit, Granola, Yogurt, Popcorn, Chips & Hummus, etc.

MEAL PLANNER

MONDAY

TUESDAY

WEDNESDAY

THURSDAY

FRIDAY

SATURDAY

SUNDAY

Notes

Remember to Get the Kids Involved in Healthy Eating & Include Them in Grocery Shopping!

- Fruit over candy
- Healthy eating over junk food
- Fast Food can be healthy too!
- Ask children what their favorite healthy foods are and add them to your list or the children's own Grocery Shopping List
- Educate children and explain why healthy foods are better for them!
- Educate children on the fact that what they eat now will determine their health.
- Educate children on the fact that what they eat now may very well affect their life span/how long they will live!

Kids Daily Meal

Breakfast

Lunch

Dinner

Snacks

Notes

Vegan Grocery List

Vegan Grocery List

Homework

<u>ASSIGNMENT DAY 6</u>

- Time to go Vegan grocery shopping!

My favorite places to purchase Vegan food is Whole Foods, Sprouts and yes...COSTCO!

Did you know Costco has great produce and great prices! Costco also carries organic produce and organic frozen fruit. I use frozen fruit for my delicious smoothies!

Albertsons, Smiths and just about all the major chain grocery stores carry a wide variety of Vegan frozen meals. Even Walmart has just about all the name brand Vegan frozen meals and organic produce.

- Become familiar with different types of produce. You can do this by simply browsing the Produce Department at your favorite grocery store.

- Subscribe to or browse some of the great Vegan magazines, which many grocery stores carry.

<u>WHAT'S FOR DAY 6 DINNER</u>?
After experiencing Transition Foods & Vegan Dining Out, which did you enjoy more? Feel free to choose from either a Transition or Dining Out.

7

RECLAIM YOUR HEALTH!

You do not need 21 days to learn to become Vegan! In fact due to the horrible health issues eating the SAD caused me, I went Vegan overnight!

And YES, you can still enjoy donuts and ice cream as long as they are Vegan. However as with anything, eating such treats as Vegan donuts, cookies and ice cream must also be done in moderation. On the flip side, some Vegan ice cream can be good for you, such as when you use healthy ingredients like avocados as an ingredient in ice cream.

EAT FOODS COMPATIBLE WITH YOUR BODY

When you begin to reclaim your health, remember that your body can heal itself (to some degree)! Of course if you should continue to see your physician if necessary.

You must unleash your body's natural healing ability by eating foods that are compatible with your body, which will allow you to activate your body's amazing healing potential.

To start your healing process, it's crucial to know that you must

- STOP doing what is causing you to feel and look sick.

- TAKE HEALTHY SNACKS WITH YOU when you run errands. If you will be gone from Home over 1 hour, toss a few snacks in a zip lock, Bento Box or the like, and take snacks with you. Taking snacks with you will avoid you stopping to get junk food. I cannot cheat or stop to even get junk food because I will have another death-defying "attack".

- USE BPA FREE CONTAINERS.

FOODS THAT SHOULD NEVER BE EATEN

MEAT

Animals, cows, pigs, chickens, turkeys, etc., are pumped full of harmful antibiotics and hormones then branded and castrated without painkillers.

When the human body breaks down protein, the liver produces uric acid, which is later excreted from the kidneys and urine. If a person eats too much meat, an excess of uric acid builds up. The build up of uric acid remains in the blood because the kidneys can't handle it, which then causes uric acid to crystallize. The body later deposits the excess urine in joints, which leads to kidney problems, arthritis, osteoporosis and other illnesses.

Meat is high in saturated fats which clogs arteries and causes heart problems, obesity, elevated cholesterol and other diseases. Did you know that pigs have so much cholesterol that in cold weather they become stiff as though they're frozen? Pigs are the only animal that develops arteriosclerosis. Pigs are also often infected with dangerous parasites which causes trichinosis.

MICROWAVE POPCORN

Olga Naidenko, PhD, a Senior Scientists for The Environmental working Group says: *"Studies show that microwaving causes the chemicals to vaporize and migrate into your popcorn. The chemicals stay in your body for years and accumulate."*

Pop natural kernels the old fashion way in a skillet. Add natural flavorings such as olive oil and dried seasonings.

FARMED SALMON

David Carpenter, M.D., Director of The Institute for Health and Environment at The State University of New York, University at Albany states: *"Nature did not intend for salmon to be crammed into pens and fed soy, poultry litter and hydrolyzed chicken feathers. As a result, farmed salmon is lower in vitamin D and higher in contaminants including carcinogens, PCBs, brominated flame retardants and pesticides such as dioxin and DDT. Preliminary science has also linked DDT to diabetes and obesity. When you eat farmed salmon you get dosed with the same drugs and chemicals, high level of antibiotics and pesticides used to treat farmed fish."*

NON-ORGANIC COCONUTS

I do NOT eat the very popular white coconuts with the cute dome top that many restaurants use and many people are seen drinking from with a straw. Here's why: Firstly, 99% of the time I eat organic food, and the majority, if not all young Thai coconuts are grown with chemical fertilizers then dipped in chemicals many times. When coconuts are dipped, workers wear protective clothing such as heavy aprons and gloves. To make sure the workers do not touch the coconuts they use long poles with wire baskets to remove the coconuts from the chemical dip.

A natural coconut husk turns brown within minutes of husking. The white Thai coconuts are dipped a last time prior to packing then wrapped in plastic for transport. During the final chemical dip, workers try to avoid touching the coconuts because they still contain trace amounts of formaldehyde.

Coconuts have a soft eye where the sprout grows to make a new tree, and chemicals can also easily enter the coconut through the soft eye.

YOU NOW HAVE THE NECESSARY KNOWLEDGE TO BE VEGAN

All you have to do is simply APPLY the principles in this book.

If you ever get a "little rusty" and need a refresher, simply return to this book, re-do the Worksheets, look up other Vegan movies, etc. However once you do the Homework in about socializing with other Vegans (see Chapter 6), being Vegan will feel very natural and you will continue to learn and thrive!

Hey...remember to stretch on a regular basis!

If you love or like this book feel free to let me know!

Have a GREAT VEGAN LIFE!

Sincerely,
Dawn Martin
cinderellavegan@mail.com

If You Want To Dress The Part!

Go Vegan

STAY HEALTHY!

STAY VEGAN!

PLEDGE

Change begins with me

I ______________________________owe it to myself, my Family, my future, health and well being to eat healthy and remain Vegan.

Maintaining my health is not up to my Family, Physician or anyone else.

Maintaining my health is up to me.

My health is my wealth.

Without my health I have very little or nothing.

Professionals can only guide me, because final decisions regarding my health are mine.

The decisions regarding what I eat now will directly affect my future.

I must stay true to my best interests.

It's not only necessary, but mandatory that I continue to eat healthy by consuming a Vegan Diet.

VEGAN

____

Date

Homework

ASSIGNMENT FOR DAY 7

- [ ] Complete Your Pledge

- [ ] Revisit Chapters 1 - 6 if necessary

- [ ] Make sure you've completed all the Homework, Worksheets, Meal Plans and Grocery Shopping Lists in this book!

WHAT'S FOR DINNER FOR DAY 7?
You tell me! You now know how to dine on Transition Foods, look up Vegan Restaurants, where and how to shop for Vegan food to prepare at Home, and how to meet other Vegans!

ENJOY THE JOURNEY BEING VEGAN!

SKIP THE DIET
just eat
Healthy

You Did It!
Congratulations

VEGANISM

Resources

Great Vegan Links!

https://doctorsaredangerous.com/

earthlings.com

happycow.net

https://mercyforanimals.org/

https://www.vegan-nutritionista.com/vegan-nutrition.html

https://www.vegansociety.com/

Product Resources

Dawns Personal Product Links!

Dawn's Juicer:
https://amzn.to/3FIKbWO

Dawn's Bento Box:
https://amzn.to/3DWXFh2

Dawn's Blender That's Still Working Great After 20 YEARS!:
https://amzn.to/3p8KAv7

Dawn's Mini Food Processor (You can get a larger size)
https://amzn.to/3p6h88L

self-care check-in

CHECK THE BOXES OF THE ACTIVITIES YOU DO TO TAKE CARE OF YOURSELF

EAT HEALTHY. EAT VEGAN!

FIND A QUIET SPOT TO RELAX

MAKE A GRATITUDE LIST

PRACTICE DEEP BREATHING

LISTEN TO GOOD MUSIC

EXERCISE

CATCH UP WITH A FRIEND

VISIT A FAMILY MEMBER

SPEND TIME OUTDOORS

HAVE A MINI PAMPER SESSION

CUDDLE A PET

TRY SOMETHING NEW

READ A BOOK

Make it a habit to take care of yourself

MY NOTES

MY NOTES

MY NOTES

Peace
love
vegan